Testimonials abou

I would recommend David Gordon to any injured person. He is fair and will not settle your case until you are happy. I am very happy with the settlement David got for me.

Mike H.
Memphis, TN

David Gordon exceeded our expectations with my wife's motorcycle injury. I highly recommend him.

David M.
Memphis, TN

David worked as hard on a small claim as if it were a million dollar loss. I hope I won't need his services again, but if I do, I'll trust no one else.

Gayle G.
Olive Branch, MS

Mr. Gordon is a true professional and a gentleman.

Joyce H.
New Orleans, LA

Mr. Gordon worked wonders. I had been offered $20,000 for my workers compensation injury, but Mr. Gordon got $37,000! Don't wait to call David Gordon.

Kenneth S.
Memphis, TN

Mine was a difficult case. We were in uncharted waters. David Gordon as a Board Certified lawyer was just the man for the task and I could not have been more pleased. His expertise was critical in order for me to receive the settlement I needed and hoped for. You can do no better than David Gordon.

Mark L.
Memphis, TN

I would highly recommend David Gordon. He returned my initial call promptly and said he'd be glad to help. Four months later he put money in my pocket.

Leslie W.
Memphis, TN

I had given up on the justice system and my trust in lawyers until I hired David Gordon.

He restored my trust in lawyers because he is so honest and fair. I feel like he went the extra mile and he always had my best interest at heart. He never made a promise to me he did not keep. He was always there when I needed him just like he'll be there for you.

Patricia V.
Olive Branch, MS

I am convinced that David Gordon takes his responsibilities to his clients very seriously. He doesn't look to his own interests, but to his client's.

Debbie Lee G.
Springfield, GA

I never thought I would be in a position to need a lawyer, but I am so thankful for a man of integrity like David Gordon. In going through my worker's compensation lawsuit, I quickly learned that he had my best interest at heart and he was able to provide me with wisdom and insight that is not easily found. I admire him and consider him a true friend.

Tony M.
Southaven, MS

When we began our lawsuit, many people told us we would never win. David Gordon did not believe that. In fact, in his representation of us, he fought through five intense years of litigation which eventually led us to a precedent setting victory in the Ninth Circuit Court of Appeals and a $150,000 settlement. Mr. Gordon is an honest and ambitious lawyer. He is also a compassionate family man who cares about people like us.

Robert and Shirley C.
Newcastle, CA

We will be eternally grateful to David Gordon for orchestrating an early settlement in our case. We were very pleased with the amount of the settlement he negotiated for us. Thanks to him, our children will now be able to go to college.

William and Mary D.
Hesperia, CA

Mr. Gordon came highly recommended to me shortly after I realized I was in need of his services following an automobile accident. His initial demeanor and poise was more than impressive, and he took the few extra moments to ensure that I was comfortable. His concern was genuine and his support was unending throughout the entire ordeal. As my first experience with any lawyer, I don't think anyone else could have made an easier transition for me than David Gordon.

Nicole P.
Memphis, TN

I would not hesitate to recommend Mr. Gordon for several reasons. He always kept me well informed on the status of my case and returned my phone calls promptly. It was obvious he spent long, uninterrupted hours working on my case. I sincerely believe Mr. Gordon is genuinely concerned about his clients and is totally committed to each individual he represents.

Rela J.
Germantown, TN

I was fortunate to choose David Gordon Law Office out of the yellow pages. I couldn't have chosen one that would have been more on top of the situation right from the start. David's attention to detail and his personal concern for my situation made the process of dealing with it a lot easier. If I had a friend who needed a lawyer, I would tell him to call the law offices of David Gordon.

David H.
Memphis, TN

On December 2, 2002, I was in a car accident. It was not my fault and I was badly hurt. The other driver's insurance company was not cooperating. I did not know who to call because I was warned that the lawyers on television have so many cases that they are slow in handling your case. My husband found David Gordon in the yellow pages.

If you are looking for the lawyer who cares about your accident, who will keep you informed, and who will promptly take care of your case, David Gordon is the lawyer for you. I made the right choice and so will you.

Lakesha N.
Memphis, TN

David Gordon got my son more money for his injury than I dreamed possible.

Alice R.
Gates, TN

I know David Gordon got me the maximum amount of money possible. He always kept his word, he really cares about his clients, and I trust him completely.

Damon K.
Memphis, TN

I've seen David Gordon in action. Not only was he personable and responsive to all my concerns, but I watched him negotiate a settlement for me that I will never forget.

Ricky R.
Southaven, MS

Mr. Gordon was patient, courteous, and kept us informed. I will use him again and I would recommend him to anyone.

Dorothy H.
Memphis, TN

Mr. Gordon put me at ease immediately. He talked to me in a language I could understand. I never felt like he was hiding anything from me, but was always honest and sincere.

Doris N.
Memphis, TN

Mr. Gordon was expedient and thorough in gaining the settlement of my case. He met with me on my schedule and gave me a secure feeling that he was doing the best job in accomplishing my goals. I would gladly recommend him to my friends and family when looking for a take charge, knowledgeable attorney who also possesses the sensitivity to Christian values.

Cheryl J.
Memphis, TN

About one year after my accident I was contacted by my insurance company offering me a small sum if I would sign a settlement agreement. It was only then that I realized I needed an attorney to advise me. David Gordon advised me that my insurance company was offering me a pittance to get me to settle. Thanks to his efforts, I received not only payment of my medical costs, but also a fair payment for my personal damages. I would recommend Mr. Gordon to anyone who needs representation by an honest attorney who will do his best for you.

George P.
Memphis, TN

David Gordon is the best lawyer in America. He has integrity, he's trustworthy, and he gets the job done.

Reggie C.
Memphis, TN

I did not have a very high opinion of lawyers before I contacted David Gordon. But he changed all of that. He kept me informed, he's honest, and he was a pleasure to work with.

Janice V.
Memphis, TN

That's one television commercial I'm glad I saw. I wrote down the phone number and I'm glad I did!

Richard B.
Memphis, TN

I needed help. Nobody else was helping me. David Gordon is a lifesaver.

Rose W.
Memphis, TN

David Gordon said he would be by my side and he meant it. He was a godsend. He really was.

Jeff M.
Memphis, TN

At that first meeting, I knew I was in good hands. He explained the process thoroughly, and by the time I left there, I was confident that my situation would be resolved. Whenever I called, he would either take my call immediately or return it very quickly. He would answer my questions with honesty and sincerity.

The most impressive part of this entire experience though, was the way he handled the mediation. Instead of dismissing my feelings or giving me lip service, he actually took my opinion. I gave him a number that I felt would satisfy me when this whole process started, and when battle was over and the smoke had cleared, he actually managed to exceed my expectations.

Rick B.
Memphis, TN

Having been badly injured in an automobile accident, I chose David Gordon to represent me. It resulted in being one of the best decisions I have ever made. I turned over to him all my fears and insecurities of "what to do next" relating to the legal complexities of the accident, which enabled me to focus on my health issues. Not only was this a tremendous relief, due to his seasoned expertise and knowledge, David Gordon gained me thousand of dollars by collecting the maximum amount on my insurance policy and keeping my expenditures to a minimum. All of this was accomplished in a superbly professional and timely manner. Thank you David Gordon!

Glenn G.
Memphis, TN

This is a non-solicited testimonial. I had worked in the printing industry for the past 25 years without an injury. All of that changed on August 25, 2003. There was an explosion and fire on the job where I was burned on 18% of my body. I really had no knowledge of workman comp so I knew I needed help with the law. My daughter made an appointment for someone from a well-known firm to come to my house and talk with me. A representative showed up at my home about a week later. When he sat down, the first thing he produced and laid out was a contract. Within a few minutes he told me I was asking too many questions, so I asked him to leave.

I started going through the yellow pages and began to make calls. I talked to everyone other than a lawyer. Then I called David Gordon. On the first call I talked with Mr. Gordon. The next day Mr. Gordon was at my home. He came in and took out a legal pad and started to take notes. When I made a statement that he did not fully understand, he stopped me and got clarification. I knew I had chosen the right man. Mr. Gordon worked hard for me. When I talked with him, there were never words of what he was going to do; it was always I think this is what **we** should do. He got me a very good settlement. David Gordon is a man of his word and a very good lawyer. I highly recommend him. I told one of my co-workers about Mr. Gordon when he was injured, and he informed me that he was also happy with Mr. Gordon. You cannot go wrong hiring Mr. Gordon to represent you.

Lonnie O.
Horn Lake, MS

I would highly recommend Mr. Gordon to anyone. He accomplished more in two weeks than my previous lawyer had done in a year.

Clarence A.
Memphis, TN

You are the best lawyer that I have ever met and I will always refer clients to you.
Your client always,

Edith K.
Memphis, TN

In past times, after a stressful week at work, I would say "TGIF - thank God it's Friday." Now, because he made it happen, after the many weeks and months of stress, I say "DGIF – David Gordon is fabulous!"

Sandra C.
Covington, TN

David Gordon is one of the best men I've ever met in my life!

James H.
Memphis, TN

It is said that David Gordon is the best lawyer in Memphis and I truly believe that.

Jimmy M.
Atoka, TN

I felt more like a family member than a client. David answered all of my questions and never made me feel dumb. Each time I called, I **ALWAYS** received a call back within the hour and was **ALWAYS** kept up to date about my case. I highly recommend his firm to my family and friends.

Vanessa J.
Memphis, TN

I just wanted to say thank you for all that you've done for my worker's compensation case and applaud the great communication, superb follow up job that Laquita Walton does. Since I have been a client of yours, it's been a very difficult time dealing with worker's comp and my injury/pain. Laquita does an excellent job on keeping me informed and that relieves tremendous amount of stress from me. Just wanted to note the superior job that you all do. And I am glad to have you & your staff handling my legal affairs. Thank you again for all that you do.

LaTraviata S.
Memphis, TN

I had been with two lawyers on previous occasions and had horrible experiences. I thought all lawyers were like that until I met David Gordon. He and his staff treated me courteously, kept me well-informed, and got a great result. I recommend him to everyone.

David P.
Memphis, TN

David Gordon restored my faith in lawyers.

Cody B.
Memphis, TN

You and your law office were always respectful, professional, and very understanding of my needs. You took the time to listen, and in today's busy world, that means a lot! May the Lord continue to bless you.

Karen S.
Memphis, TN

19 THINGS YOU MUST KNOW (AND THAT THE INSURANCE COMPANY WON'T TELL YOU)

19 THINGS YOU MUST KNOW (AND THAT THE INSURANCE COMPANY WON'T TELL YOU)

If You've Been Injured In Tennessee or Mississippi

DAVID E. GORDON, ESQ.

ISBN: 1523433639
ISBN 13: 9781523433636

PREFACE

I wrote this book to help injured people navigate the dangerous waters of an injury claim. Initially, it was shocking to me that insurance companies were so deceptive in their dealings with the injured, even when those people were their own policyholders. I'm accustomed to their ways now, but I know that the public is not, so I've tried to arm the reader with enough information to keep him from getting skinned. Remember, most lawyers will discuss your case with you for free. If you have not yet reviewed your claim with a lawyer, we encourage you to do so with us. If you already have a lawyer, we hope this book will help you maximize your case.

TABLE OF CONTENTS

Chapter 1

THE OTHER DRIVER'S INSURANCE ADJUSTOR IS NOT ON YOUR SIDE.

Despite what you may hear from TV advertising, insurance companies are not on your side when you make a claim for injuries. They are quick to take your premium, but slow to pay your claims. To be fair, the claim adjustor's job is to minimize payment. Premiums must exceed claims if they are to make a profit. So when the friendly adjustor calls you after the wreck, promising to "take care of you," know that what she really means is "take advantage of you."

* Do Not Expect to Be Treated Fairly

The other driver's company is not obligated to inform you of your rights or to treat you fairly. There is not a Tennessee or Mississippi law requiring insurance companies to educate injured people concerning their rights. Do not expect an insurance adjustor to explain to you that you have separate claims for 1) lost earnings, 2) pain and suffering, and 3) loss of enjoyment of life. Do not expect an insurance adjustor to inform you of the strict time limits that apply to your claims, known as statutes of limitation that are discussed later in this book. And then finally, do not expect their settlement proposal to be fair. There is no review of the settlement by a judge or state agency. Once you sign the settlement release, the case is over.

There are a number of ways the adjustor takes advantage of you. The first is by getting from you what is known as a "recorded statement." A recorded statement is as the term implies - a taped interview. By recording the interview, the insurance company can use what you say against you in the event this case goes to trial. That's right, even in that first conversation with the insurance adjustor, he or she is already making plans to gain ammunition against you in the event you decide to retain a lawyer and someday file a lawsuit.

- **Do Not Permit the Opposing Insurance Adjustor to Record Your Statement**

One of the first items on the opposing insurance company checklist is to obtain your recorded statement. In this statement the insurance adjustor will interview you about how the accident occurred and about your injuries. The adjustor may lead you to say things that are harmful to your claim, so it is important that you **refuse** to have your statement recorded. In fact, you should not permit an interview at all if the police report is accurate. Just tell the adjustor that the police report is accurate and he can rely on it.

There are a number of pitfalls into which you can fall during one of these recorded statements. The first one is on the subject of liability. Remember, your claim is valid only if the accident is not your fault. Imagine you were injured when another driver turned into your path as you traveled straight through an intersection. Suppose you tell the adjustor that you were "going the speed limit" when he asks you how fast you were going as you entered the intersection. Then when he asks you for the speed limit, you guess and say "I think it is 45 M.P.H.," when in fact, the speed limit is 35 M.P.H. The insurance adjustor now has a recording of you admitting that you were speeding at the time of the accident! Your claim is now in big trouble.

Here is another example. In this instance, imagine that the other driver emerged from a commercial driveway on your right. You struck the other vehicle broadside as it crossed your lane. Because the accident was only two days before, you are now suffering headache and dizziness and are not thinking clearly. When the adjustor asks you how fast you were going, you say that you "do not remember." When he asks you how far from the other vehicle you were you when it emerged from the driveway, you again say that you "do not remember." Even if your mind should clear within a few days and you then recall that you were traveling slowly and that you were only a few car lengths from the driveway when the car pulled out, you have given a statement that may crush your claim. Here's why. If the other driver says that you were approximately 100 yards away when he pulled out and that he then noticed you coming at a high rate of speed, you are not in a position to rebut this evidence because you said you "do not remember." Even without a witness, the insurance adjustor now has evidence that you contributed to this accident and may, in fact, be at least 50% fault.

Statements made regarding your injuries can also come back to haunt you. Because it is not unusual for pain to increase over the first 72 hours following an accident, you may tell the adjustor in that recorded statement on the day following the accident that you are "okay" or that "you just feel a little shaken up." When your first medical visit is three weeks after the collision because you had to wait for an appointment, the insurance company is going to use that statement you made as evidence that your torn rotator cuff (shoulder muscle) is not a result of the accident, but was pre-existing.

Under the terms of your own automobile policy, you are required to cooperate. This includes the giving of a recorded statement, so you will have to comply with your company if requested to do so.

* **Do Not Permit the Opposing Insurance Adjustor to Have Your Medical Authorization**

In addition to your recorded statement, another item on the opposing adjustor's checklist is your medical authorization. This is a written document that if signed by you will allow the insurance company to get unbridled medical information on you. **Do not let them have it**. By obtaining your medical authorization, the insurance adjustor has the opportunity to search your medical records for pre-existing injuries and any other medical issues you may have, including those that are unrelated to the accident.

Of course, if you are handling your claim without a lawyer because your injuries are minor or for some other reason, you will be required to sign a medical authorization unless you can obtain the relevant records and bills on your own. The insurance company must have your medical information, including the bills, in order to evaluation your claim. So you must either sign the medical authorization so they can obtain the documents, or get them yourself for the insurance company.

Chapter 2

COMPENSATION FOR INJURIES IS ONLY AVAILABLE IF THE ACCIDENT WAS NOT YOUR FAULT.

Fault is the first issue that every insurance adjustor and every lawyer must address. This is because compensation for bodily injury is only available in Tennessee if the accident was less than 50% your fault. In Mississippi, your claim will be reduced by whatever percentage of fault is assigned to you. As we described above, the insurance adjustor for the other driver is always trying to find something that you did wrong to contribute to the accident. If the insurance adjustor thinks you are 25% at fault, then your claim will be reduced by 25% in both Tennessee and Mississippi. If the adjustor finds you 50% at fault, your claim will be denied in Tennessee and cut in half in Mississippi.

Because this issue is so important, it is vital that you do everything in your power to preserve and present the evidence that is favorable to you. For example, suppose you are injured in an intersection crash in which the other driver turned left into your path as you attempted to cross through the intersection. You know your light was green, but the other driver tells the police officer he had a green turn arrow. This is the kind of claim that will be denied unless you have a witness. So do **everything** you can to get the name, address, and phone number of witnesses. They may be critical to your case.

The same is true of an accident in which the oncoming vehicle is speeding into the intersection on a red light while the turning driver attempts to clear the intersection. The turning driver has a chance, especially in Mississippi, if she can prove that the other driver was speeding and that the light was red. But without a witness, the turning driver's claim is dead on arrival.

Photographs at the scene can also be helpful. In a case in which each driver claims that the other driver came into his lane and thereby caused the collision, a photograph of the other vehicle pressed against your vehicle in your lane will resolve the dispute! This is also true regarding head-on collisions where each driver blames the other. The photograph does not lie.

Chapter 3

COMPENSATION FOR INJURIES IS RELATED TO THE SEVERITY OF THE INJURY AND THE SIZE OF THE CRASH.

It may seem surprising that the extent of the property damage has a relationship to the compensation for one's injuries. Many people believe that if they have been in an accident, then they are entitled to be compensated. But insurance companies know that juries in 2016 are not impressed with injury claims when the property damage is slight. They know that juries will not award much, if anything, for pain and suffering following an accident in which there is very little damage to the vehicles. For example, if a rear-end collision does not produce damage because the two vehicles met at the bumpers, which are designed to give a little upon impact, then juries are deaf to complaints of injury. Therefore, when the property damage is small, the recovery for the injury is likely to be small.

The flip side of this coin is also true – if the car is crunched like an accordion, then juries are listening to the cries of the injured. Because of this fact, insurance companies put more value on claims arising from severely damaged vehicles. This is the reason that photographs of your severely damaged vehicle are so important.

* **What Types of Damages Can You Collect After a Car Accident?**

Remember: Every car accident claim is unique. The compensation you can recover will depend on a variety of factors such the extent of the property damage that occurred and whether you were partially at fault for the accident.

Because the circumstances present in your accident can determine which losses you can recover, you might not be entitled to recover every type of damage. This is an issue to discuss with your attorney during your first meeting with him or her.

The personal injury harms and losses that car accident victims typically can recover include:

MEDICAL EXPENSES

Medical bills can be very expensive. These bills include your diagnosis, hospitalization, and treatment costs. After you have received your initial diagnosis and treatment, you could be required to continue taking medication and going to physical therapy sessions. These costs, too, can be part of your medical expenses claim.

To prove your need for compensation for your medical expenses, you must provide copies of the medical records and bills. The doctor's notes must connect the treatment to the car accident, so it is important that you are clear with your physician on your first visit following the crash. Be sure to tell him or her about the collision and the symptoms you experienced since it happened.

LOST WAGES

When you suffer a significant injury, you may have to spend time out of work to focus on your recovery. During this time, you are missing out on both wages and opportunities for career advancement. Both of these are considered when determining an appropriate amount of money to compensate you for your lost wages as a result of your injury.

In order to prove your lost wages claim, you must provide a statement from your employer indicating the dates, hours, and hourly rate you missed from work. These three items must be on your lost earnings statement from your employer. If a lost promotion is a part of your claim, you will need evidence to prove that you were close to promotion. For instance, you can include recommendations from your supervisor and a copy of your company's advancement schedule. A work excuse from your doctor will also be necessary to correspond with the time missed due to your injuries.

PAIN AND SUFFERING

Pain and suffering refers to the physical and mental ways in which you suffer after an accident. Physical pain like headaches and neck pain is expected for several weeks following most accidents, so insurance companies are ready to give at least a modest amount of compensation for it. But if the pain continues for several months, or perhaps longer, then there must be medical evidence to corroborate it. In other words, your physician's notes must reflect your complaints of pain and your need for treatment. A positive x-ray or MRI lends credence to your claim for an extended period of pain and suffering.

Suffering can refer to your need for psychological counseling to work through any mental issues that stem from your accident, such as depression or anxiety about driving again.

LOSS OF ENJOYMENT OF LIFE

Loss of enjoyment of life is compensation for the isolation that many times occurs following a serious crash. We are social creatures, so being trapped in one's home, unable to go to work, unable to go out at night, unable to go on vacation, etc. are losses that are compensable if properly presented. Particular losses like organized athletics, hunting, dancing, etc., are important if they are activities that the injured individual enjoyed regularly before the collision.

DISFIGUREMENT

In the event the individual suffers an injury that results in permanent disfigurement, such as scarring, there is a separate category of compensation for this loss. The amount of compensation due will depend upon the extent of the disfigurement, whether it is visible when the individual is fully dressed (i.e. hands or face), and the age of the victim (i.e. the injury to a young person is greater than to an older person because he or she must endure it longer).

WRONGFUL DEATH DAMAGES

In Tennessee and Mississippi, unique types of damages may be pursued when a car accident caused by another results in the wrongful death of a loved one. These damages generally include medical costs, funeral bills, and compensation for the conscious pain and suffering and loss of enjoyment of life that your loved one experienced between the time of injury and the time of death.

Additionally, in a Tennessee or Mississippi wrongful death claim, you can seek the "pecuniary value" of your loved one's life. Speaking in general terms, this amount represents what he or she would have earned over his or her expected lifetime minus his or her projected expenses.

If the victim was one's spouse, you can also typically seek damages for the loss of their affection and companionship. Similarly, a child can seek damages for the loss of a deceased parent's love, security, and guidance.

Chapter 4

CALL YOUR INSURANCE COMPANY, EVEN IF THE ACCIDENT WAS NOT YOUR FAULT.

In Tennessee, about 20 percent of the drivers sharing the road do not have current auto insurance, and the state ranks sixth in the number of uninsured drivers. The likelihood of being hit by one of these drivers is exceptionally high in the Memphis area. If you discover the other driver did not carry any auto insurance, your own insurance must be accessed to recover compensation for your injuries and property damages. Although you may have religiously paid your premiums, don't expect that your own insurance company will make it easy to recover compensation for your injuries.

Reporting the accident to your own company will not result in a premium increase or a cancellation of your policy unless the accident was your fault. Even if the other driver has insurance, it will oftentimes be several days, or even a week, before the other driver's company accepts responsibility for the accident. This means that you will not have access to a rental, nor can you begin to see about your car's repair, for that length of time. If your car is disabled, you may want to initiate a claim through your company so you can get a rental and get your car repaired. Your insurance company will then get reimbursed from the other driver's company.

A secondary bonus from filing the claim with your company is that you get their help in reaching the other driver's company. Your company wants to be reimbursed for its payments on your claim, so it is motivated to find that other company and get the reimbursement process moving forward.

The only downside from making a claim against your company in this situation is that you probably have a deductible on your collision coverage and copay on the rental. But if you need a car, it is worth it. Any deductible and copay charged to you will be reimbursed when your company is reimbursed by the other driver's company.

Chapter 5

CALL THE RESPONSIBLE DRIVER'S INSURANCE COMPANY, EVEN IF THEY DO NOT CALL YOU.

If they don't call you, call them. If you don't know the name of the insurance company, call the other driver to find out. If you don't know the name of the other driver, get the police report from the department who investigated the accident. Memphis, Germantown, Bartlett, and Collierville Police Departments have separate locations for accident reports. Similarly, each town in Northern Mississippi has a police department that maintains the reports. Now the reports from most cities and towns are available online. These reports have the name of the other driver's insurance company, as well as his/her policy number.

Sometimes a driver at the scene of an accident does not have his insurance card with him. In this instance, the driver will be ticketed and there will be no insurance information on the report. Therefore, you will have to call the driver to get his information. His phone number should be on the report.

Chapter 6

GET MEDICAL TREATMENT AS SOON AS YOU ARE AWARE OF THE SLIGHTEST INJURY.

Many personal injury lawyers advise people to get "checked out" after every accident, regardless of whether they are aware of injury. We advise our clients to get treatment as soon as they are aware of any injury.

Many times a person's adrenaline will protect him from immediate pain, but within hours of the accident, there is muscle soreness and spasm. It is so important that you get treatment for that pain. You may have an injury that is only a muscle strain, but it is also possible that you have a herniated disk in your neck or a torn rotator cuff muscle in your shoulder. **The longer you wait before getting treatment, the greater the argument you give the insurance company that your condition is not a result of the accident.** When you delay getting treatment, insurance companies call this a "gap" in treatment and they will use it to cast doubt on your claim.

Many people think they will be denied treatment at a hospital ER if they do not have health insurance. Federal law, however, prohibits the refusal to provide medical treatment at hospital emergency rooms. You will incur charges, but treatment must be provided.

Chapter 7

YOU ARE ENTITLED TO A RENTAL CAR OR $ FOR "LOSS OF USE."

While your car is being repaired, or until you receive a check for the total loss, you are entitled to a rental car from the other driver's insurance company. You will be responsible to insure the car, so use your automobile insurance for that purpose. Your policy contains a provision to insure a "substitute vehicle," which is what a rental car is in this situation.

If you do not obtain a rental from the other driver's company because you have another vehicle available to you, you are, nevertheless, entitled to money for what is called "loss of use." Loss of use is payment to you because your car was disabled and you did not have access to it. It is calculated on a daily basis over the same period of time as it would take to repair your vehicle or settle the total loss claim. You must request this payment because **the insurance adjustor will not otherwise offer it to you**.

Chapter 8

YOU ARE ENTITLED TO THE FAIR MARKET VALUE OF YOUR VEHICLE.

Property damage is based upon what is called the fair market value of the vehicle. Fair market value is the amount of money that a willing buyer would pay a willing seller in your market. The fair market value has nothing to do with what you paid for the car (unless you purchased it within a few days of the accident) or how much you owe on the car.

Fair market value does, however, include such items as a recently rebuilt engine, a new transmission, new tires, or an after-market sound system, etc. If you can show receipts for such items, you are entitled to a higher fair market value.

The fair market value is usually determined by a guide in the possession of the insurer. So you should do your own research by checking guides such as N.A.D.A. and AutoTrader.com. If you can show the insurance adjustor that vehicles like yours are selling for more in your city than he offered, you may be able to get an increase in his offer.

The fact that your vehicle was financed and there is a balance on the loan is not relevant to the property damage calculation. If your vehicle is a total loss, even if there is a balance after the fair market value is figured, there will be no additional payment to the finance company. That balance will still be your obligation unless you purchased what is called "gap insurance" at the time your vehicle was purchased.

Chapter 9

YOU SHOULD GET A FREE CONSULTATION WITH A LAWYER IF YOU'VE BEEN INJURED.

Insurance companies do not want you to hire a lawyer. That's because they know they will have to pay a larger settlement if you are represented by a lawyer. **The Insurance Research Council found that the settlement figure was 3 and 1/2 times higher for individuals with lawyers.** Statistics prove you benefit and the consultation is free!

It is possible that your injuries are not serious enough to justify the services of a lawyer. Claims for minor injuries that include little more than an emergency room visit or a couple of visits to a physician are not likely to result in much more than compensation for the medical bills. If you pay the attorney one-third of the settlement, you may actually receive less than if you had handled the claim yourself. But consult an attorney about this. Remember, the consultation is free, so you have nothing to lose by inquiring.

Immediately after being seriously injured in an accident, you are "thrown" into an adversarial legal system. In other words, the insurance company representing the party at fault for the accident has in place a team of adjustors, investigators and attorneys who are working against you seeking to pay as little as possible to settle your claim.

Many accident victims, already in distressed physical and financial circumstances, understandably choose to delay the "hassles" involved in selecting and hiring a personal injury attorney. Others having had a "bad experience" with an attorney (i.e. divorce) or simply do not like or trust attorneys on "general principles," attempt to represent their own legal interests.

Almost all injury lawyers work on what is called a contingency basis; that is, they are paid only if they make a recovery for their client. This is usually based upon a fraction of the recovery, such as one-third. **If there is no recovery, then there is no fee owed.**

The bottom line is that considering the complexity of the established system for compensating accident victims, the hiring of a qualified personal injury attorney is often a "necessary evil" to "level the playing field" and to ensure that you receive maximum compensation for your injuries.

Chapter 10

IF YOU ARE INJURED WHILE DRIVING A COMPANY VEHICLE, YOU HAVE TWO INJURY CLAIMS.

Suppose a local route driver is injured in an accident while on his way to make a delivery. First, it is important to know that worker's compensation benefits apply, even if the accident is the employee's fault. If the accident is not the employee's fault, then the injured worker should **also** be compensated by the other driver. Worker's compensation applies, but the driver at fault is also obligated to pay the injured worker like any other injured motorist; namely, for medical bills, lost earnings, pain and suffering, and loss of enjoyment of life. (Remember, however, that if you get paid by the negligent driver, the workers' compensation insurance company is entitled to reimbursement for everything it previously paid).

In the event of a serious injury, the claim against the other driver for your pain and suffering and loss of enjoyment of life will be the larger claim. Workers compensation benefits in TN and MS have been pared down by the state legislatures, resulting in very little money for even permanent injuries. So the victim of a car wreck at work should consult a lawyer to see whether he can be compensated fully through an automobile insurance claim.

It is possible in this situation that your own automobile insurance policy will provide compensation to you even though you were injured in a company vehicle while at work. This would be the case if the other driver is uninsured and you have uninsured motorist coverage on your policy.

Chapter 11

THERE ARE 10 EASY WAYS TO MAXIMIZE YOUR CLAIM.

A. WRITE DOWN EVERYTHING THAT HAPPENED

Shortly after the accident, everything is fresh in your mind. But with each passing day, your memory of the events fades. For example, it is common for a driver to be apologetic at the scene of an accident, to explain that he was "in a hurry," that he "was late," or that "he didn't see you." These are important admissions if the other driver's insurance company decides to deny coverage and blame you for the accident. So write down everything that happened at the scene, including exactly what was said by all drivers.

You should also write down how the accident happened. The weakest ink is stronger that the greatest memory. For example, write down the length of time you waited at the intersection before being struck, or the approximate distance from the other vehicle you were when you saw him emerge from the driveway on your right and into your path. Write down your estimate of your speed, as well your estimate of the other driver's speed when applicable.

If you were hurt on the job, write down how the accident occurred, as well as the names of the witnesses and the name of every supervisor you informed. If you were injured as a result of faulty equipment, record all of the details about the product, including the manufacturer and serial number, if possible. If a safety engineer or supervisor made a comment about the failed product, write it down! **You cannot record too much information.**

B. KEEP A DIARY OF YOUR PAIN AND DISCOMFORT

In addition to your medical bills and lost earnings, the driver at fault is responsible for your physical pain and suffering, and for your loss of enjoyment of life. Because it could be several months, or possibly years, before you are asked to describe the impact of the injury on your life, a written record is essential.

Keep a daily record of headaches, insomnia, medications taken, pain suffered, etc. And don't forget to keep up with activity you previously enjoyed, but in which you cannot now participate (i.e. exercise, golf, dancing, automobile trips, etc.). Events you miss such as a vacation, a wedding, children's sporting events or recitals, should also be recorded.

Mental suffering is also something you should be compensated for, so record your discouragement, sadness, and frustration that is related to your rehabilitation process. The feelings of social isolation and depression that come from long periods of being trapped at home are common, so don't be ashamed of them. Record it!

C. TAKE PICTURES

You know that a picture is worth a thousand words. So it should come as no surprise that photographs of the damaged vehicles and of your physical injuries are powerful witnesses. Take lots of pictures throughout your rehabilitation and date them for later use. Photos of you in the hospital bed and afterward in your orthopedic boot or neck brace can be valuable pieces of evidence of the severity of your injury.

D. TELL YOUR DOCTOR ABOUT EVERYTHING THAT HURTS

The doctor's office is no place to be a hero. Your doctor (or nurse assistant) is trained to record everything you complain of and everything else you say related to your condition. For example, he records your comment that you "feel pretty good today" or that you are "much better." Likewise, he makes a note when you tell him that you "can't sleep" or that "it hurts whenever you roll over in bed." When the doctor's records are provided to the insurance company of the other driver, these notes are important. If the doctor is asked to testify on your behalf, these notes are critical because the doctor will rely heavily upon them. If you contend that your shoulder was keeping you awake at night for two months after the accident, but you never told your doctor about it, the claim is questioned. On the other hand, the doctor can powerfully corroborate every complaint you are making if you properly inform him during the course of your treatment.

E. FOLLOW THE DOCTOR'S ORDERS

Your doctor's records will reflect exactly what limitations and instructions he gave you. And the other driver's insurance company will almost always see these records eventually. If they can find evidence that you did not obey your physician, then they can justify paying you less. For example, if the doctor told you to stay off work for a week and you returned in three days, then you can be held responsible for your slow recovery. Similarly, if he prescribed an exercise regimen that you ignored, then you will be blamed for the lingering problems.

F. BUILD A GOOD RELATIONSHIP WITH YOUR DOCTOR

After you, your doctor will be the single most important witness on your behalf. If he likes you, it is only natural that he will want to help you with his testimony. It is possible that your physician will be asked whether your condition is a result of the accident or some other cause. He may also be asked how long your condition can be expected to last. It is only natural that your relationship with him will affect the way in which he responds.

If he found you abrasive or argumentative, his testimony will be nothing more than the reading of his office notes.

G. GET WORK EXCUSES FROM YOUR DOCTOR

Lost earnings are an important element of the compensation due to an injured person. But the injured individual must connect the work absences to his injury. Even if your employer does not require written excuses, a note from the physician will be valuable when you are later trying to prove that your absences were the result of the injury.

H. KEEP DOCTOR'S APPOINTMENTS

Missed appointments are kept in the doctor's records. They are blemishes on your character and the authenticity of your need for medical treatment. Do everything you can to keep your appointments or call to reschedule.

I. DON'T EXAGGERATE

Nothing can sink an injury case faster than false testimony. Many times the injured party is not lying, but is only exaggerating slightly the extent of the injury. For example, the injured individual tells the insurance company or the other attorney that because of his pain he can no longer take automobile trips and has not taken one since the accident. Yet the doctor's notes reflect that he drove to Florida over spring break with his family. Another example is a person who claims he can no longer play sports with his son, yet a private investigator has a video of the man in squatting position catching a child's 70 m.p.h. fastball. These cases are doomed, despite the fact that a significant injury was suffered.

J. BE PATIENT

The insurance adjustor is trained to show you courtesy and concern in an effort to minimize your claim. His effort to win your confidence is aimed at one goal – to keep you from retaining legal counsel and thereby be required to pay you **all that you are owed.** Any payment for your pain, suffering and loss of enjoyment of life is tempting, but you must be patient. You only get one payment for the injuries that you may suffer for the rest of your life. A lawyer with personal injury expertise will guard your right to be fully compensated.

Chapter 12

MEDICAL EXPENSES SHOULD BE PAID BY YOUR HEALTH INSURANCE CARRIER OR AUTOMOBILE INSURANCE CARRIER.

Many injured people expect the other driver's insurance company to pay their medical expenses as they are incurred. But the other driver's insurance will not do so. Instead, the other driver's insurance company will wait until you finish all of your medical treatment. At that time it will review all of your bills to determine if the charges are what it deems reasonable and necessary. Insurers today are refusing in almost every instance to pay the full medical charges, claiming that the charges are too high.

Because the other driver's insurance is not going to pay for your medical treatment, it is important that you submit your bills to your health insurance provider. Sometimes, the medical provider (i.e. hospital, doctor, etc.) will want you to first submit the bill to your automobile insurance company. In that case, if you have what is called "Medical Payments" coverage, your auto policy will pay the medical charges up to the amount of your coverage. When your automobile medical coverage is exhausted under your policy (usually $5,000 or less), then the health insurance will begin to pay the bills.

If the passengers in your car are injured in an accident, your "Medical Payments" pays their medical bills, usually up to an amount such as $5,000. These payments are made regardless of whose fault was the accident. **Insurance companies are not quick to advise their insureds who have been injured that they have this coverage, so it is important that you know about it.**

Chapter 13

YOU CAN GET TREATMENT FOR INJURIES EVEN IF YOU DO NOT HAVE HEALTH INSURANCE.

As was stated previously, many people think they will be denied treatment at a hospital ER if they do not have health insurance. Federal law, however, prohibits the refusal to provide medical treatment at hospital emergency rooms. You will incur charges, but treatment must be provided.

Second, even though lawyers are forbidden by the ethical rules governing them from paying for client medical expenses, experienced lawyers can find medical treatment for their clients. There are a number of physicians, including specialists like orthopedists and pain management doctors, who will treat a lawyer's client in exchange for the lawyer's promise to pay him or her from the settlement. Lawyers can find these doctors for their clients.

The importance of this cannot be overstated. Many injured people are not getting the treatment they need because they are concerned about the cost. They have neither health insurance nor the ability to pay out-of-pocket for the treatment, so they get none. In the meantime, their physical condition worsens and they will end up getting neither the medical treatment nor the personal injury compensation that they deserve.

For the past 10 years or so, chiropractic hustlers have been preying upon people injured in Mid-South accidents. These crafty agents pretend to be representatives of high sounding companies like "Advocates for the Injured" or "Mid-South Injury Center," but in reality, they are nothing more than people trying to hustle injured people into their chiropractic clinic by twisting information and making promises they cannot keep. Most insurance companies are aware of these practices and some refuse to pay claims involving their medical treatment. Run from these clinics like your pants are on fire.

Chapter 14

IF THE OTHER DRIVER DOES NOT HAVE ENOUGH INSURANCE TO COVER YOUR CLAIM, THEN YOU SHOULD ALSO MAKE A CLAIM UNDER YOUR POLICY.

Tennessee law requires only that motorists have $25,000 of liability of coverage. If the driver who injures you has only a minimum limits policy ($25,000), then this is the maximum that his insurance company can be forced to pay. Any additional payments will have to be made by the driver himself, which are very difficult to obtain. To add to the difficulty against the driver personally is the fact that the insurance company will not pay you until you release in writing your rights against the responsible driver.

But you do have another important option. Your uninsured motorist coverage (UM) may apply here. Uninsured motorist coverage is actually referred to as "underinsured" motorist coverage in this instance. If you have $50,000 of Uninsured/Underinsured coverage, then even if the other driver has only $25,000 of liability coverage, you will be covered up to $50,000. Your insurance company gets credit for the liability payment by the other driver's company ($25,000), but it is responsible for the part of the claim that is greater than $25,000, up to $50,000. Naturally, if you have $100,000 or $250,000 of UM coverage, then the potential benefit to you in this situation is even greater.

And remember, there is a state law against raising your premium or cancelling your policy for a claim that is not your fault. So making a UM claim cannot hurt you!

Chapter 15

STATUTES OF LIMITATION ARE STRICTLY ENFORCED AND CANNOT BE IGNORED.

The Tennessee statute of limitation is one year and the Mississippi statute of limitation is 3 years. This means that a claim for physical injury resulting from an accident must be resolved within that time or a lawsuit filed to preserve the victim's legal rights. These statutes of limitation are strictly enforced. Do not allow an insurance adjustor to lull you into believing that "everything is going to be taken care of," even though the one year or three year anniversary is approaching. Many injured people have received nothing because they thought the insurance company could be trusted. They were waiting for the adjustor to call them with an offer when the statute of limitation expired. There is nothing that can be done at that point. When you get to within 60 days of the expiration of the statute of limitation, you should contact a lawyer. Then the burden is upon him/her to see that your rights are protected by the filing of a lawsuit if necessary.

Chapter 16

RESEARCH INDICATES THAT PEOPLE WITH LAWYERS GET MORE MONEY FOR THEIR INJURY.

Research and experience have revealed that lawyers negotiate settlements 3 ½ times higher than unrepresented individuals.* This means that even after paying the lawyer his percentage of the settlement, the injured person has more than he would have gained on his own.

When an injured person first consults a personal injury lawyer, one of the first things this client would like to know is how much the case is worth. An experienced personal injury lawyer can usually give a broad range of value at the first meeting. The lawyer knows that the individual is entitled to be compensated for the following:

1) Physical pain and suffering
2) Mental or emotional pain and suffering
3) Loss of the normal pleasures of life
4) Disfigurement (scarring)
5) Medical expenses
6) Loss of earnings

But a good lawyer would never try to answer this question with certainty, however, until he has completed a full investigation into the accident, all the damages and expenses have been totaled, and the client's doctors have reported how the injury will affect the client in the future. Often it is several months after the accident before all the necessary factors are known which will enable the lawyer to evaluate the claim and begin settlement negotiations with the insurance company. If the client insists on a quick settlement, this can be accomplished, but almost always the client will get less than the full value of the claim. Another danger of settling too soon is that an unknown injury may appear weeks or months later. If the claim has been settled and the responsible party released, it cannot be reopened.

At The Law Office of David E. Gordon we endeavor to settle every claim for "top dollar". We are not a personal injury "mill" which sacrifices full value in favor of quick and easy settlements. That is, we deal in quality, not in quantity.

We make every effort to achieve a full and fair settlement before we resort to filing a lawsuit in court. Because David Gordon is board certified, insurance companies know that he has the experience and skill to file a lawsuit if the settlement is too low. This usually results in a fair settlement for our client without a lawsuit. Our goal is always the same: To achieve the maximum recovery for our client.

*Insurance Research Council – 1999 study

Chapter 17

PERSONAL INJURY CLAIMS ARE OFTEN SETTLED WITHOUT GOING TO COURT.

Most cases are settled before it is necessary to file a lawsuit. And then even after filing a lawsuit, most cases are settled prior to trial. Generally, only the large cases or highly disputed cases end up being tried before a jury or judge. Our extensive experience allows us particular foresight in determining what process will be the most advantageous to you. Whatever the situation, we will discuss all available options with you.

Like most businesses, insurance companies exist to make money. The simple fact is that the less money it pays out to settle claims, the better an insurance company's profit margins are. For something like a minor fender bender, it may be in one's best interests to deal directly with the insurance company. Property damage assessment is fairly standardized within the auto industry and is oftentimes based on a quote from an auto body shop or an insurance agency representative. A claims adjuster may offer you fair compensation just to avoid dragging out the case and incurring further expense to his employer. However, when your claim involves significant personal injury, the case becomes much more complicated.

In response to a personal injury claim, an insurance company may offer a sum of money up front, wanting to settle the claim immediately. If the victim has no legal representation, and, likely, little knowledge of the value of the personal injury claim, it is doubtful that the adjuster will make a reasonable offer. The insurance company is hoping that the victim will take the money and thereby relieve them of any additional financial responsibility. Once a claim has been settled, the claimant has legally released the defendant from further payment, even if the victim's condition worsens.

An early settlement is often unfair when an individual has suffered what may be a permanent injury. When a person has a scar, for example, or required surgical repair of an ankle or shoulder, the result is a permanent injury. One who suffers a permanent injury is entitled to be compensated for his physical pain or his loss of enjoyment of life over the entire course of his life. In other words, a person who is 40 years old when injured can anticipate suffering from the condition for another 40 years. The settlement amount must reflect that fact and it rarely, if ever, does when an individual elects an early settlement without a lawyer.

A personal injury attorney is there to protect the interests of the client. An experienced lawyer, especially one who concentrates on personal injury law, has years of experience in the field and has a good idea of what a given claim should be worth. The personal injury attorney can collect evidence to support the case, file the necessary paperwork, and speak directly with the insurance companies or opposing lawyers. Perhaps most importantly, hiring a personal injury attorney lets the insurance companies know that the claimant is serious. A personal injury lawyer represents the threat of a costly lawsuit, which the insurance company wants to avoid. Most personal injury cases will be resolved by a settlement rather than going to court. On the other hand, a personal injury attorney should be prepared to take the case to trial if a fair personal injury settlement is not reached; otherwise, the adjuster won't respect the threat of a lawsuit.

The length of time it takes to settle a case depends largely on the severity of the injuries. Each case is different. Generally, however, settlement negotiations will begin after you reach what doctors call "maximum medical improvement." It is at this time that doctors ordinarily release their patients. We will gather your medical records and bills to present them to the insurance company with a settlement demand. The length of the negotiation process varies among insurance companies and according to the severity of your injuries. Cases involving relatively minor injuries are usually resolved within 30 days of making a settlement demand. Larger cases usually take longer to settle.

If it is necessary to file a lawsuit to protect your rights, it takes much longer to reach agreement. Delay is caused by a variety of factors:

* The litigation process itself requires a lengthy discovery period during which the sides exchange information
* Crowded court dockets
* Difficulty in obtaining medical documentation
* Difficulty in obtaining testimony from witnesses

These and other factors play a part in how quickly a case can be resolved. Taking a case to trial, in general, takes a long time. Settlement, mediation, or arbitration may significantly speed up the resolution of a case.

Your case should never be settled without your approval. At The Law Office of David E. Gordon, we discuss every valid settlement offer with you, and no settlement offer will be accepted without your approval.

We will make recommendations to you and try to clearly explain the reasons for the recommendations. Because we have extensive experience in settling cases and are familiar with what juries and judges generally award in similar cases, our recommendations can be trusted.

Chapter 18

STORE OWNERS, HOMEOWNERS, AND LANDLORDS ARE SOMETIMES RESPONSIBLE IF YOU GET HURT ON THEIR PROPERTY.

If your injury is the result of a dangerous condition about which the store owner knew or should have known, then it is liable for your injuries. For example, if you fall in the restroom that has just been mopped by the cleaning staff, there is liability if there were no warning signs. On the other hand, if you slip in the aisle of a department store, it will be difficult to prove that the store knew or should have known about the small puddle of water or other beverage on the floor.

In these situations, it is vital that you write down the name of any employee who indicated to you that they knew about the dangerous condition. If an employee says, "I was on my way to clean that up," or "I knew we should have done something about that," then he is admitting knowledge of the dangerous condition and you need evidence of that. So write it down, along with the employee's name.

Like the store owner, the homeowner is only liable for injuries resulting from a dangerous condition that he knows about or should know about. An unmarked hole in the yard or a broken step is something that could result in liability. Homeowner's insurance usually provides for payment of medical bills incurred as a result of injury on the premises, but nothing more unless there is negligence as described.

Like the store owner and the homeowner, the landlord is only responsible for a dangerous condition that he knows or should know about. What makes this case especially difficult is the fact that a tenant who has lived in an apartment for any length of time may also know about a dangerous condition and is thereby equally responsible for the injury.

Chapter 19

A BOARD CERTIFIED LAWYER GIVES YOU AN ADVANTAGE.

Less than 2% of Tennessee lawyers are board certified. Certification is important to you because it assures you that specific lawyer's skills, integrity, and experience have been carefully scrutinized by a national board of experts and found to be exceptional. The certified lawyer knows how to handle insurance companies that are trying to pay you as little as possible. And equally important is the fact that the insurance companies know that a board certified lawyer has the skill and experience to take the case to trial if the offer is unfair.

The National Board of Legal Specialty Certification, or NBLSC, was created in the public interest to identify lawyers who demonstrate that they are skilled, capable, ethical trial lawyers.

In the area of medical services, we are all familiar with board certification of physicians. When we see that a doctor is board certified, we know that the doctor has been tested and examined by an independent group of physicians who have verified that the doctor is properly qualified and skilled in his or her field of practice.

Accredited by the American Bar Association, the National Board of Legal Specialty Certification maintains rigorous standards for the certification of civil, criminal, and family law trial advocates.

The U.S. Supreme Court affirmed NBLSC's mission and purpose, finding that "Information about certification and specialties facilitates the consumer's access to legal services and thus better serves the administration of justice." The Supreme Court went on to say that the NBLSC's certification "both serve the public interest and encourages the development and utilization of meritorious certification programs for attorneys" *Peel v. Attorney Registration and Disciplinary Commission of Illinois,* 110 S.CT. 2281 (1990).

* WHAT MUST A LAWYER DO TO BE "CERTIFIED" ?

1. They must submit a list of names of judges and lawyers who are contacted by the NBLSC to independently verify the lawyer's skill, experience and even the lawyer's reputation for ethical and professional conduct.
2. They must establish that they are in good standing with their state bar association.
3. They must pass a day-long written examination.
4. They must submit actual copies of their written legal work for review.
5. They must provide documentation to prove their active involvement in multiple trials before judges and juries.

In order to keep his certification active, the lawyer must obtain continuing legal education and remain in good ethical standing with the bar association.

Every National Board of Legal Specialty Certification attorney has met, and continues to meet, NBLSC's rigorous standards for certification illustrating nothing less than:

* High Ethical Standards
* Extensive Experience in the Designated Specialty
* Hefty Participation in the Development of Law and Continuing Legal Education
* Outstanding Peer and Judicial Commendations
* Demonstrated Practical Skill in the Designated Specialty

* **WHY SHOULD IT MATTER?**

Why should it matter to you whether your lawyer is a board certified trial lawyer? You want your case resolved without having to go to trial.

Virtually 98% of civil cases never actually go to trial. This is because they are settled out of court.

What will motivate your opponent to want to settle with you out of court? If you are represented by an experienced trial lawyer who is making a reasonable request for settlement on your behalf, the opposition knows it would probably be foolish to take the case to trial against an experienced, skilled litigator.

On the other hand, if the opposition knows something you don't know – that your lawyer has virtually no experience in court or has demonstrated a serious lack of skill in court – the opposition is much less likely to meet your settlement demands because they feel confident about their chances of success against your lawyer in court.

For these reasons, the most powerful advantage you can have is a lawyer who is known to be a highly-skilled trial lawyer. The odds are much greater that such a lawyer will be able to successfully negotiate an out-of-court settlement for you.

Litigation is often times compared to war. In litigation, as in war, the side with the greatest skill and experience is usually able to avoid conflict because the opposition is not willing to risk the consequences against such a capable opponent.

Therefore, as strange as it may seem at first, your chances of successfully resolving your case out of court are much better when you are represented by a skilled, experienced trial lawyer who is well-known and respected by the opposition. The NBLSC simply makes these lawyers known to the public by identifying them as "Board Certified by the National Board of Trial Advocacy."

ABOUT THE AUTHOR

David Gordon is a highly reviewed personal injury lawyer in Memphis, TN. He is one of less than 2% of Tennessee lawyers that are Board Certified by the Tennessee Supreme Court. He has received a perfect rating of 10.0 by AVVO, an independent service that rates lawyers. David has an AV rating of pre-eminent, the highest rating that the prestigious Martindale-Hubble reviewers give.

He has also been named a Super Lawyer in 2006, 2011, 2012, 2013, 2014, and 2015, which includes less than 5% of Tennessee lawyers. David has a perfect A+ rating by the BBB (Better Business Bureau) Business Review and has been practicing law for 33 years, specializing in personal injury for the last 14 years.

In recognition of his legal accomplishments, the Memphis Bar Association and The National Business Institute have had David conduct numerous continuing legal education seminars for local lawyers since 2002.

David and his wife, Julie, have six grown children and live in Memphis.

For a free consultation, contact David Gordon at:

The Law Office of David E. Gordon
1850 Poplar Crest Cove, Suite 200
Memphis, Tennessee 38119
901-818-4889
TheMemphisLawyer.com
Davidg@DavidGordonLaw.com

Made in the USA
Columbia, SC
17 February 2025